THE COLORADO MOUNTAIN CLUB

Pocket Guide to the
Colorado 14ers

D1021258

THE COLORADO MOUNTAIN CLUB
Pocket Guide to the Colorado 14ers

A Project of
The Colorado Mountain Club Foundation,
edited by Ania Savage

Johnson Books

BOULDER

Published in the United States by Johnson Books, a division of Johnson Publishing Company, 1880 South 57th Court, Boulder, Colorado 80301.

9 8 7 6 5 4 3 2 1

Cover photograph of Crestone Needle by Jim Gehres

Library of Congress Cataloging-in-Publication Data
The Colorado Mountain Club pocket guide to the Colorado
   14ers / edited by Ania Savage.
        p.   cm.
   Includes index.
   ISBN 1-55566-204-8 (alk. paper)
   1. Mountaineering—Colorado—Guidebooks. 2.
Mountains—Colorado—Guidebooks. 3. Trails—Colorado—
Guidebooks. 4. Colorado—Guidebooks. I. Savage, Ania. II.
Colorado Mountain Club.
GV199.42.C6C65   1997
917.88'0433—dc21   97-17570
                                                    CIP

Printed in the United States by
Johnson Printing
1880 South 57th Court
Boulder, Colorado 80301

  Printed on recycled paper with soy ink

CONTENTS

COLORADO
Roads and 14,000' Peaks
KEY

1.	Mount Elbert	14,433
2.	Mount Massive	14,421
3.	Mount Harvard	14,420
4.	Blanca Peak	14,345
5.	La Plata Peak	14,336
6.	Uncompahgre Peak	14,309
7.	Crestone Peak	14,294
8.	Mount Lincoln	14,286
9.	Grays Peak	14,270
10.	Mount Antero	14,269
11.	Torreys Peak	14,267
12.	Castle Peak	14,265
13.	Quandary Peak	14,265
14.	Mount Evans	14,264
15.	Longs Peak	14,255
16.	Mount Wilson	14,246
17.	Mount Shavano	14,229
18.	Mount Princeton	14,197
19.	Mount Belford	14,197
20.	Mount Yale	14,196
21.	Crestone Needle	14,191
22.	Mount Bross	14,172
23.	Kit Carson Peak	14,165
24.	El Diente	14,159
25.	Maroon Peak	14,156
26.	Tabeguache Mtn.	14,155
27.	Mount Oxford	14,153
28.	Mount Sneffels	14,150
29.	Mount Democrat	14,148
30.	Capitol Peak	14,130
31.	Pikes Peak	14,110
32.	Snowmass Mountain	14,092
33.	Mount Eolus	14,083
34.	Windom Peak	14,082
35.	Mount Columbia	14,073
36.	Culebra Peak	14,069
37.	Missouri Mountain	14,067
38.	Humboldt Peak	14,064
39.	Mount Bierstadt	14,060
40.	Sunlight Peak	14,059
41.	Handies Peak	14,048
42.	Mount Lindsey	14,042
43.	Ellingwood Peak	14,042
44.	Little Bear Peak	14,037
45.	Mount Sherman	14,036
46.	Redcloud Peak	14,034

47.	Pyramid Peak	14,018
48.	Wilson Peak	14,017
49.	Wetterhorn Peak	14,017
50.	North Maroon Peak	14,014
51.	San Luis Peak	14,014
52.	Huron Peak	14,005
53.	Mount of the Holy Cross	14,005
54.	Sunshine Peak	14,001

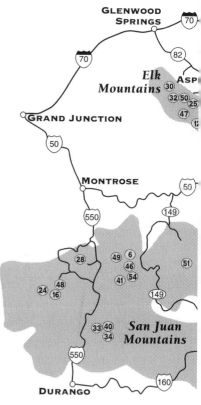

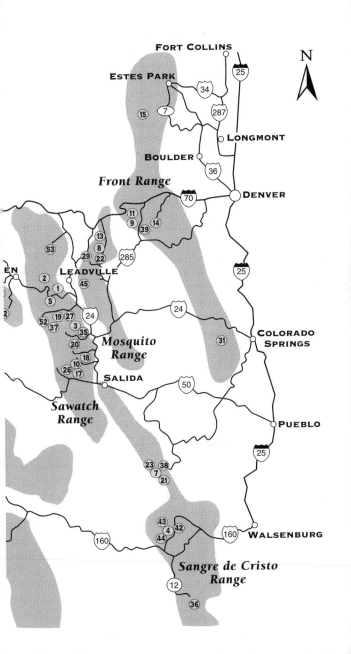

INTRODUCTION

The *Pocket Guide* offers the latest information on accessing and climbing Colorado's 54 peaks that exceed 14,000 feet—in a lightweight, pocket-carrying size.

Mountains change little in our lifetime, but access to them does. This *Pocket Guide* lists the most popular routes to the Fourteeners and indicates changes in trails that have been made in recent years. The *Pocket Guide* also advises you about the routes recommended by the Colorado Fourteeners Initiative. This cooperative effort of governmental agencies and hiking groups was formed in 1994 to protect Colorado's highest peaks by standardizing routes and promoting minimum-impact hiking and backpacking.

Climbing the Fourteeners

The Fourteeners stretch across Colorado, from Longs Peak in the Front Range, in sight of Wyoming, to Culebra Peak, just north of New Mexico, and to the San Juan Range near the famous Four Corners area where Colorado, Arizona, New Mexico and Utah meet. Climbing the Fourteeners will take mountaineers to many parts of Colorado and introduce them to a variety of flora, fauna and rock.

"How many Fourteeners are there?" is a question that has intrigued climbers since the early days of exploration. A guide published in 1925 lists 47. Included in this ranking are Stewart Peak in the San Juan Range and Grizzly Mountain in the Sawatch Range, which later were demoted to Thirteeners. Missouri Mountain and its neighbor, Huron Peak, were added to the list in the mid-1950s, after new measurements by the US Geological Survey (USGS) were made. Mount of the Holy Cross appeared on the list, was taken off, then reinstated. By 1972, 53 peaks were recognized as Fourteeners. Ellingwood Peak in the Sangre de Cristo Range was the last peak to be added to the list. Today, 54 mountains are recognized as Fourteeners, both by the USGS and by the Colorado Mountain Club (CMC).

The organization of the *Pocket Guide* is straightforward. The peaks are grouped by the ranges in which they are found, and listed from east to west across Colorado. Within each range, the peaks are cited from north to south. The climbing routes are for summer and early autumn trips. Winter conditions can alter not only the route but also the entire climbing experience. Distances given are round trip distances except when noted otherwise.

The directions, however, cannot be relied upon as a substitute for good judgment and careful preparation. The guide makes no provision for the many variables that affect a climb, such as weather, physical condition of the participants and the possibility that climbers will fail to locate the described landmarks.

Climbers should use this guide with discretion and awareness of the countless hazards and challenges that must be confronted on even the "easiest" climbs. High mountains are subject to abrupt and drastic weather changes. Afternoon lightning storms should always be expected when climbing the Fourteeners from April to September, and some peaks do seem to have more storms than others. These peaks are so identified in the text. Due to the frequency of early afternoon storms, summer climbs should be planned so that the party is descending from the summit by noon.

Despite what anyone may tell you, breathing almost three miles above sea level or climbing several miles upward at a high altitude will not only take your breath away, it will tire you quickly. The more serious physical discomforts climbers may encounter are nausea, headache and, occasionally, heart palpitations. There is an inherent risk in climbing mountains, and each climber attempting a Fourteener should be aware of the risk. For this reason, the three climbers who have so generously shared their knowledge of Colorado's Fourteeners in the *Pocket Guide* maintain that there is no really "easy" mountain. Slippery cliffs, falling rock, crumbling ledges, heaving talus slopes and abrupt changes in the weather can turn a pleasant hike into a difficult climb. Thus, none of the mountains is ranked "easy," and we do tell you if a mountain is difficult and if the climb can be dangerous.

High altitude almost always means low temperatures and strong wind. Therefore, frostbite and hypothermia are possible dangers. Climbers can become exhausted or lost, or they may find themselves facing cliffs requiring technical rock-climbing skills. The consequences of climbing beyond your ability not only expose you to injury but also endanger those hiking with you or coming to your assistance if you cannot go on.

We climb to challenge the limits of our body and to test our capacity for risk. Yet, to go unprepared—carry no maps or compass, take an inadequate amount of water, or eschew a pack with warm clothing and rain gear—is foolhardy. On a Fourteener, a cloudless sunny day can rapidly change to a snowstorm or a whiteout. Drinking unpurified stream water can expose you to waterborne parasites.

The 10 Essentials

A hiker properly equipped will more likely than not have a successful outing. Essential equipment includes broken-in hiking boots over wool socks on your feet and an extra pair or two of socks, wool and nylon, in your pack; quick-drying pants, not jeans; a lightweight, wool or man-made-fiber shirt; a hooded jacket or parka; warm head covering; rain poncho and plenty of water, plus at least one meal.

The CMC has adopted a list, compiled by The Mountaineers of Seattle, of the "10 essentials" that hikers and mountain climbers should carry in their backpacks. These essentials are:

1. Map
2. Compass
3. Flashlight or headlamp
4. Extra food
5. Sun protection—hat, sunglasses, sunscreen
6. Extra clothing
7. A small first aid kit
8. Pocket knife
9. Matches
10. Fire starter

If you think you cannot carry the extra weight, perhaps you should re-consider your decision to climb a Fourteener in the first place. Some of the peaks require the use of helmets, a rope, and occasionally ice axes. Climbers attempting these mountains should be familiar with belay and self-arrest techniques. It is also imperative that you tell a friend or a family member where you are going, and sign in at the trailhead if a register is available.

"Leave No Trace" Hiking

The Fourteeners are a harsh yet fragile environment. Above timberline, plants grow at the outer edge of life on Earth. Even slight human disturbance can cause long-term damage. Impacted areas may take hundreds, if not thousands, of years to recover.

To minimize environmental impact, the hiker should remain on the trail, especially in those areas where trail modifications have been made to reduce human impact. Because of the increased popularity in climbing the Fourteeners, ascents on weekdays not only minimize human impact but also offer solitude and diminish trail and campground congestion.

Leave No Trace (LNT) is a national program that promotes and inspires responsible outdoor recreation and suggests six basic principles for hiking and backpacking:

- Know the regulations, inherent risks and special concerns for the area you'll visit.
- Use existing trails and don't cut across switchbacks.
- Carry out all trash, including used or left over food.
- Properly dispose of what you can't pack out. Deposit human waste in holes dug 6 to 8 inches deep, at least 200 feet from water, camp and trails. Carry water 200 feet away from streams and rivers for washing.
- Leave what you find. Leave plants, rocks and historical artifacts as you find them. Keep dogs under control at all times.
- Use a campstove. Where fires are permitted, use established fire rings, fire pans or mound fires.

Mountaineering in Colorado

An arrowhead found on the boulder field below the summit of Longs Peak and a man-made shelter discovered at the apex of Blanca, yield evidence that Native Americans did climb Colorado's great mountains. Members of several surveys, especially the Hayden and Wheeler surveys, climbed many of the Fourteeners. A survey team climbed and named Mount Harvard and Mount Yale in 1869, while Mount Massive and Mount Elbert were summitted in 1874. Trappers and miners also climbed some of the great mountains, and prospect holes were found near the summits of Handies Peak and Mount Bierstadt, while abandoned cabins and mines dot the flanks of Mount Democrat and Mount Lincoln. Early climbers discovered evidence that grizzly bears may have used the summits of several peaks as habitat. A she grizzly "came rushing past us," reported a climber nearing the summit of Uncompahgre Peak in 1874. Claw marks were also discovered on the rock near the summit of Sneffles. The first record of someone climbing all of the then-known Fourteeners in Colorado dates to 1923 when Carl Blaurock and William Ervin achieved this feat. In 1912, Blaurock was one of the charter members of the CMC, whose history is intimately tied to the exploration, mapping and even naming of Colorado's mountains. Today, the CMC has more than 9,000 members.

The Colorado Mountain Club

The CMC began placing registers on the peaks of the Fourteeners in the 1910s and 1920s. Old registers, which are available to researchers, are archived in filing cabinets at the American Mountaineering Center in Golden, Colorado. Registers from the early years of the twentieth century show that the number of climbers scaling the Four-teeners remained fairly constant until the 1950s. Climbing increased in popularity in the 1960s and 1970s, and exploded in the 1980s and 1990s. On a popular mountain such as Longs Peak, a regis-ter with room for 500 signatures fills in a week. Registers are rolled up and stored in PVC plastic canisters secured at the summit by a cable or rock. Sometimes it is difficult to find the small, incon-spicuous gray tube. Once you locate the canister, sign your name with a ballpoint pen or with a pencil. Signatures made with a felt-tip pen tend to bleed on the entire register and obliterate names.

CMC members have also produced several mountain guides to Colorado's Rockies. The most exhaustive guide is the ninth edition of _Guide to the Colorado Mountains_. A number of detailed and useful guides to the Fourteeners by intrepid mountaineers in and outside the CMC are also available. These books are invaluable resources when planning ascents of the most difficult peaks. John L. Jerome Hart wrote the first history of the naming and early ascents of the Fourteeners in 1925. As climbing the Fourteeners grew in popu-larity, Hart's guide was reprinted in 1931 and up-dated in 1972. A new guide, based on Hart's but containing specific routes, was prepared in 1967 by Ray Phillips, another active CMC member. This guide was revised in 1978 by Sally Richards, as the editor, with Jim Gehres and Al Ossinger preparing many of the updates. Jim and Al, as well as Giles Toll, are responsible for the latest trail updates in this _Pocket Guide_. These three men, avid mountaineers and CMC members, have climbed the Colorado Fourteeners numerous times. In fact, if all their climbs—in the United States and abroad—are compiled, the number of their ascents stands at more than 1,100, a remarkable achievement. This *Pocket Guide* would not exist without their input.

The Colorado Mountain Club Foundation

The Colorado Mountain Club Foundation (CMCF) was created in 1973 and supports expeditions to such far-flung places as the Himalayas and China. Since 1981, the CMFC has given grants to students in college and graduate school doing research on the history, geology, geography, biology and other aspects of Colorado's mountains. The CMCF also provides loans to the Wilderness Land Trust to permit the purchase of land when it becomes available in areas where trail access is restricted. The CMFC publishes brochures to educate hikers on hypothermia, lightning and snow avalanche, and it distributes these materials free of charge to hikers through the CMC, the Forest Service, the Park Service and sporting goods stores. The CMCF also maintains a list of those who have climbed all of the Fourteeners. At the time of publication, the list contains almost 1,000 names. Individuals active in the CMCF volunteer their time. Contributions to the CMCF are tax deductible. All royalties from this Pocket Guide will benefit the work of the CMCF.

Climbers interested in the work of the CMC and the CMCF may obtain further information by contacting the club and the foundation at the American Mountaineering Center, 710 Tenth Street #200, Golden, CO 80401. Climbers who have completed the 54 Fourteeners should notify the Colorado Mountain Club Foundation at the above address to register their accomplishment and be included in the annual listing of those who have completed the Fourteeners. Remember, an unwritten rule of the CMC is that a valid climb of a Fourteener entails an elevation gain of at least 3,000 feet. As with many rules, there are exceptions and the 3,000-foot-gain rule per peak does not apply when you are climbing two adjacent mountains, or where the access trail begins at a higher elevation, such as Mount Bierstadt.

Logistics

Unfortunately, the increase in private land ownership in the Colorado high country has become a limiting factor in many mountain hikes. However, as of the publication date of this volume, hikers have unrestricted access to 53 of the 54 Fourteeners. At this time, access to Culebra Peak costs $40 per person and requires approval by the owner of the Taylor Ranch. The summits of two other mountains, Kit Carson and Mount Sherman, are privately owned, but the owners permit free access to climbers.

The USGS quadrangle maps given with the peaks are 7.5 minute. They are available at some sporting goods stores or through the USGS Map Sales Office, Building 810, Federal Center, Denver, CO 80225; phone (303) 236-7477. Ice axes and climbing helmets can be purchased in sporting goods stores.

A few telephone numbers may be helpful. In Colorado, the Park Service line is (303) 234-3095. The Forest Service number is (303) 234-4187. Information about the Leave No Trace program is available by calling (303) 442-8222 or (800) 332-4100. The CMC number is (303) 279-3080. The Colorado Fourteeners Initiative numbers are (303) 715-1010 or (800) 925-2220.

Ania Savage, editor

The Front Range

(6 fourteeners)

Longs Peak

Grays Peak

Torreys Peak

Mount Evans

Mount Bierstadt

Pikes Peak

Longs Peak—14,255 feet

Map—Longs Peak 7.5 M
Rating—Very difficult
Elevation gain—4,850 feet
Round-trip distance—16 miles
Estimated round-trip time—12 to 15 hours
Nearest town—Estes Park

Drive south from Estes Park 10 miles on Colorado 7, then 1 mile west to a "T" junction. The left fork leads to the Longs Peak Ranger Station and parking lot, which is often crowded. The right fork leads to the Longs Peak Campground, where sites are available on a first-come basis. Additional camping is available at back-country sites, where permits are required. The trailhead for Longs is next to the ranger station. Follow a good, moderately steep trail 6 miles west to the boulder field at about 12,800 feet.

The Keyhole Route

Continue west for about 1 mile to the keyhole ridge at 13,100 feet. From here, the route is well marked with yellow and red bull's eyes (otherwise known as fried eggs). Follow the route onto the ledges along the west side of the peak, up the rock through to the ledge junction, or spur. Turn southwest through the "narrows" to the "homestretch" of slab rock. Then continue to the large, flat summit. This is a long, tedious climb. There is exposure on the ledges, and the upper mountain can be dangerously slick with ice. Before starting, check with the ranger regarding conditions. At certain times, an ice axe may be needed.

Grays Peak—14,270 feet

Torreys Peak—14,267 feet

Map—Grays Peak 7.5 M
Rating—Moderate
Elevation gain—3,000 feet to 3,600
Round-trip distance—8 to 9 miles
Estimated round-trip time—6 to 8 hours
Nearest town—Silver Plume

These two peaks can be climbed in one day with a little more effort than it takes to climb only one. Weather, of course, can be a factor in deciding whether to attempt both peaks. Usually, Grays, the peak to the east (left), is climbed first. After summiting Grays, the climber then proceeds to the saddle between Grays and Torreys and climbs the latter peak. Climbers starting early can drive from Denver and return to the city that same evening.

From Denver, drive west on I-70 to Bakerville, Exit 221. Turn left over the interstate and drive south 3.5 miles on a steep but wide and passable dirt road to the vicinity of Stevens Mine at 11,300 feet. There is a parking lot for about 30 vehicles, and latrines are adjacent to the parking lot. Take the iron bridge across the stream and follow a good trail that switchbacks upward for 3.5 miles. At about 13,500 feet, the trail forks. The climber has the choice of continuing up another 0.5 mile to the summit of Grays or taking the trail west to the saddle between Grays and Torreys at 13,700 feet and climbing Torreys' ridge to the summit.

After climbing Grays, descend from the summit northwest 600 feet into the saddle on a marked trail and follow the ridge north for 0.5 mile to the summit of Torreys. The distance between the peaks is about 0.5 mile as the crow flies. There is usually an extensive snowfield in the spring and early summer at the saddle. Pass to the left (west) of the snowfield, and proceed with caution.

From Torreys, return to the saddle, then work back to the trail down the north side of Grays. Early in the season, this route may entail a climb well up Grays' slope to avoid the usual snow cornice.

You may see mountain goats during the climb.

Mount Evans—14,264 feet

Map—Mount Evans 7.5 M,
   Idaho Springs 7.5 M
Rating—Moderate
Elevation gain—3,000 feet
Round-trip distance—9 miles
Estimated round-trip time—7 hours
Nearest town—Georgetown

The climb can be done in a day trip from Denver. Take I-70 west to Georgetown. From Georgetown drive south 11 miles along South Clear Creek Road to Guanella Pass at 11,669 feet. Mount Evans is hidden by a shoulder of the Sawtooth.

From the summit of the pass, hike east through the willows—which can be boggy—staying to the south of a pond, and heading for a grove of pines, using the saddle of Mount Spaulding and Gray Wolf as a guide. At mile 2, the northwest ridge end of Mount Evans comes into view to the southeast. Climb southeast across tundra above cliffs to the rough ridge, 4 miles from Guanella Pass. Rock scramble along the ridge for 0.5 mile to the summit of Mount Evans. This scramble involves some route finding and can be slow and tedious.

The peak can be hiked also on the Mount Evans Road, which can be reached by exiting I-70 at Idaho Springs. Follow road signs. To gain the required 3,000 feet in altitude, start from the parking lot at the 3-mile marker on the Mount Evans Road. A climb from Echo Lake is also possible. You may also start from Summit Lake, but from there you will not gain the required 3,000 feet in altitude.

- To hike up the road, simply follow it up to the summit, or else follow one of the many trails that appear along the road.
- To climb from Summit Lake, hike northwest around the lake to the slope, then scramble up to Mount Spaulding and follow the ridge south to the west face of Mount Evans. Scramble to the summit across a rock field.
- Continue on the road for approximately 0.5 mile above Summit Lake, then climb straight up for the summit.

Since there is a paved road to the summit, there is no register.

You may see mountain goats during the climb, especially below Summit Lake or on the Sawtooth Ridge between Mount Evans and Mount Bierstadt.

Mount Bierstadt—14,060 feet

Map—Mount Evans 7.5 M
Rating—Moderate
Elevation gain—2,900 or 3,900 feet
Round-trip distance—6 to 8.5 miles
Estimated round-trip time—6 to 8 hours
Nearest town—Georgetown

From Georgetown drive south 11 miles along South Clear Creek Road to Guanella Pass at 11,669 feet. The peak is in view to the east-south-east.

Hike southeast 1 mile through the willows on a good trail to a crossing of Scott Gomer Creek. The trail continues east, climbing 1 mile to the ridge of the peak, then following the ridge 1 mile to the summit.

Mount Evans and Mount Bierstadt Combination

The Sawtooth Ridge connecting Bierstadt to Mount Evans is exposed and is difficult if you are not experienced with rock. Do not attempt this route unless you are confident of your abilities. Consult more detailed guides if you plan to do this climb. Be especially watchful of the weather.

Pikes Peak—14,110 feet

Map—Pikes Peak 7.5 M
Rating—Moderate but long
Elevation gain—7,400 feet
Round-trip distance—26 miles
Estimated round-trip time—12 to 14 hours,
    or more
Nearest town—Manitou Springs

The town of Manitou Springs is overwhelmed by tourist activities in the summer. To camp, backpack and spend the night at one of the excellent sites along the Barr Trail. You can also stay indoors at Barr Camp, located at 9,800 feet.

To reach the Barr Trail, drive to Manitou Springs and locate the City Hall. Proceed west on US 24 (business) about 0.5 mile to Ruxton Avenue. Turn left on Ruxton Avenue and drive 0.75 mile to the Pikes Peak Cog Railroad depot, then on for a short distance to the hydroelectric plant and Hydro Street. Look for the Barr Trail parking lot and park here, if there is room. Pick up the Barr Trail trailhead. The trail switchbacks and climbs steeply for 3.5 miles, then rises gradually for the next 2 miles. After passing the 5-mile mark you will see Barr Camp. After Barr Camp, the well-maintained trail climbs steeply to the summit. Pikes Peak is a very long climb—26 miles. Since there is a shelter house and much tourist activity at the summit, there is no peak register. Before starting, you may wish to inquire at the cog railroad about the possibility of taking the train down from the summit.

Or:

- Drive up Pikes Peak Highway and park at 11,000 feet, then take odd trails near and along the highway to the summit.
- Climb up the west side of the peak from the Crags Campground near the town of Divide. The trailhead is located at the campground and the trail crosses the Pikes Peak Highway at mile 16. The road can be avoided by continuing up the ridge to the summit.

Sangre de Cristo Range

(9 fourteeners)

Kit Carson Peak

Humboldt Peak

Crestone Peak

Crestone Needle

Mount Lindsey

Little Bear Peak

Blanca Peak

Ellingwood Peak

Culebra Peak

Kit Carson Peak—14,165 feet

Map—Crestone Peak 7.5 M
Rating—Very difficult
Elevation gain—3,500 feet
Round-trip distance—7 miles
Estimated round-trip time—8 hours
Nearest town—Westcliffe

From Westcliffe drive southeast 4.5 miles on Colorado 69 toward Walsenburg. Turn right (south) for 5.5 miles to the end of Colfax Lane, then turn right. You are now heading straight west toward the Crestones. After about 1 mile the road becomes rugged, but four-wheel-drive vehicles can be driven further, sometimes another 5 miles, depending on conditions. From the turn off from Colfax Lane, it is 7 miles to South Colony Lakes at 11,700 feet. Camp near the end of the jeep road or at South Colony Lakes, which can be reached by backpacking up a closed road.

Hike northwest from South Colony Lakes on the trail along South Colony Creek to gain the ridge between Humboldt Peak and Crestone Peak at 13,200 feet. From the saddle head west along the ridge and over Kit Carson's false summit to the true summit.

Humboldt Peak—14,064 feet

Map—Crestone Peak 7.5 M
Rating—Moderate
Elevation gain—2,400 feet
Round-trip distance—4 miles
Estimated round-trip time—5 hours
Nearest town—Westcliffe

From Westcliffe drive southeast about 4.5 miles on Colorado 69 toward Walsenburg. Turn right (south) for 5.5 miles to the end of Colfax Lane, then turn right. You are now headed straight west toward the Crestones. After about 1 mile the road becomes rugged, but four-wheel-drive vehicles can be driven further, sometimes another 5 miles, depending on conditions. From the turn off from Colfax Lane, it is 7 miles to South Colony Lakes at 11,700 feet. You may camp near the end of the jeep road or at South Colony Lakes, which can be reached by backpacking up a closed road

CFI Recommended Route

From South Colony Lakes hike northwest on trail up South Colony Creek to the east side of Upper South Colony Lake. Follow a climbers' trail north up scree and talus to Humboldt's west ridge. Reach the ridge just east of the 12,850-foot connecting saddle between Humboldt and Crestone peaks. Climb east on the ridge for less than a mile to the summit.

Crestone Peak—14,294 feet

Map—Crestone Peak 7.5 M
Rating—Very difficult, climbing helmet, rope,
   & ice axe needed
Elevation gain—4,300 feet
Round-trip distance—6 miles
Estimated round-trip time—9 to 11 hours
Nearest town—Westcliffe

From Westcliffe drive southeast about 4.5 miles
on Colorado 69 toward Walsenburg. Turn right
(south) for 5.5 miles to the end of Colfax Lane,
then turn right. You are now headed straight west
toward the Crestones. After about 1 mile the road
becomes rugged, but four-wheel-drive vehicles
can be driven further, sometimes another 5 miles,
depending on conditions. From the turn off from
Colfax Lane, it is 7 miles to South Colony Lakes
at 11,700 feet. You may camp near the end of the
jeep road or at South Colony Lakes, which can be
reached by backpacking up a closed road.

Follow the trail west past Lower South Colony
Lake, then past Upper South Colony Lake to a
high plateau at 13,000 feet, called "Bear's Play-
ground." The plateau is between the Crestones
and Kit Carson. Head south up jumbled rocks to
gain the steep, red couloir that culminates near
the summit. Careful—there is residual ice on the
couloir well into the summer, and an ice axe may
be required. Falling rocks present another hazard.
Climbing helmets are necessary for safety.

Crestone Needle—14,191 feet

Map—Crestone Peak 7.5 M
**Rating—Very difficult, climbing helmet &
  rope needed**
Elevation gain—2,700 feet
Round-trip distance—3 miles
Estimated round-trip time—6 hours
Nearest town—Westcliffe

From Westcliffe drive southeast about 4.5 miles
on Colorado 69 toward Walsenburg. Turn right
(south) for 5.5 miles to the end of Colfax Lane,
then turn right. You are now headed straight west
toward the Crestones. After about 1 mile the road
becomes rugged, but four-wheel-drive vehicles
can be driven further, sometimes another 5 miles,
depending on conditions. From the turn off from
Colfax Lane, it is 7 miles to South Colony Lakes
at 11,700 feet. You may camp near the end of the
jeep road or at South Colony Lakes, which can be
reached by backpacking up a closed road.

This peak, once considered unclimbable, was
the last of the Colorado Fourteeners to be summitted. The various routes up the east face are
technical climbs. Though it is a good climbing
precaution to carry ropes, the west face, over
sound rock, can, with care, be climbed unassisted.

Circle Lower South Colony Lake to the south
and west. Climb southwest to the saddle between
Crestone Needle and Broken Hand Peak. Continue northwest along the ridge towards the
Needle. About 0.2 mile above the first bench,

angle slightly right and look for cairn-marked zigzag route on grass shelves. This route leads to the third pinnacle northeast of a low point on the ridge. Drop slightly into a narrow couloir and climb abruptly up to the summit. Look for the cairned route and follow it in your descent. Otherwise you may find yourself on a cliff overhang and will have to climb back up or use rope.

Mount Lindsey—14,042 feet

Map—Mosca Pass 7.5 M, Blanca Peak 7.5 M
Rating—More difficult
Elevation gain—3,600 feet
Round-trip distance—10 miles
Estimated round-trip time—8 hours
Nearest town—Westcliffe

Two miles north of Walsenburg, Colorado 69 intersects Interstate 25 at Exit 52. Take Colorado 69 for 25 miles to Gardner. Approximately 2 miles west of Gardner take the left fork onto an unmarked county road. Drive for 13 miles, passing the town of Redwing. Take the left fork onto Forest Service Road 407 in the San Isabel National Forest and continue 4 miles to a sign identifying the private property of Singing River Ranch. Park in an area downstream of the private property sign. The next 7 miles to the road's end can be rough and are best suited for pickup trucks and four-wheel-drive vehicles.

From the end of the road, hike 1.5 miles on an old jeep road to the upper end of a marsh area. There are excellent campsites along this jeep road. Turn to the southeast and climb up drainage to a large, grassy basin, southwest of the Iron Nipple. Stay to the left (northeast) side of the drainage. You may intersect an old trail that is not shown on most maps. From the grassy basin climb southeast to a ridge running southwest by northeast. Once on the ridge, climb northeast as needed to reach the main northwest edge of Lindsey. Once on this ridge, climb southeast to the summit. Follow the top of the ridge from the saddle to the summit. At approximately 13,400 feet, a cleft in the ridge offers difficulty over one quite short, steep point. Beyond that point this route is not difficult. Descend using the same route.

An approach from the south via Ute and Little Ute Creeks is prohibited because the land is private property. The owners do not give permission to climbers to cross the property at this time.

Little Bear Peak—14,037 feet
Blanca Peak—14,345 feet
Ellingwood Peak—14,042 feet

Map—Blanca Peak 7.5 M, Twin Peaks 7.5 M
Rating—Very difficult, climbing helmet needed
Elevation gain—2,300 to 3,200 feet from
  high camp
Round-trip distance—4 to 8 miles from
  high camp
Estimated round-trip time from high camp—
  6.5 to 8 hours from high camp
Nearest town—Blanca

Little Bear, Blanca and Ellingwood
from Lake Como

From US 160, 6 miles west of Blanca and 15 miles
east of Alamosa, drive north on Colorado 150 for
3 miles to a rough road going east. Take this road.
This road becomes progressively rougher and can
damage a car. Drive as far as possible, then pack
in to Lake Como at 11,700 feet. Camp at the east
end of the lake or higher, near timberline.

Little Bear Peak

Continue for 0.3 mile past the lake on the jeep
road. In the flats southwest of Blue Lakes, head
southwest to an obvious couloir that leads to
Little Bear's west ridge. Take the ridge until it
becomes steep and jagged. Turn right (south) and
contour for about 0.25 mile to a steep couloir that

heads directly toward the summit. This is a hazardous climb. There are many steep slabs and loose rock and a climbing helmet is a must. The time needed to climb only Little Bear from a high camp is about 6.5 hours and the distance is 4 miles.

Blanca Peak and Ellingwood Peak

Hike northeast up the basin, passing north of Crater Lake, to the Blanca-Ellingwood ridge. On the ridge, turn right (south) to ascend Blanca, or left to reach Ellingwood. Return to the saddle to descend. The time required to climb each peak is 5 to 6 hours. Both can be done in 8 hours. The distance is 6 miles for one peak, 8 miles for both.

Culebra Peak—14,069 feet

Map—Culebra Peak 7.5 M,
  El Valle Creek 7.5 M
Rating—More difficult
Elevation gain—3,000 feet
Round-trip distance—5 miles from high camp
Estimated round-trip time—6 hours
Nearest town—San Luis

From San Luis drive south and southeast on Colorado 152 through the town of Chama. The road turns east and is paved for 4 miles beyond Chama where it crosses two bridges that are a few hundred feet apart. Immediately past the second bridge make a sharp right turn and follow the dirt road about 1 mile to where the road ends in a "T" junction. Turn left, then continue to bear right and drive 2 miles more. The Taylor Ranch will be visible on your left. Stop at ranch headquarters and pay an access fee. Park here or go on for another mile but realize that the road becomes a long, steep ascent.

After leaving the ranch keep right at the first junction, take the center fork where the road branches at timberline. Follow this road to where it crosses the creek. Camp here. The distance from the ranch to the campsite is 4 miles.

From camp, ascend the ridge at the low point to the east. Follow the ridge south then southwest. Culebra's summit becomes visible at the highest point south of the ridge. Continue south then southeast on the ridge. There is a small loss in elevation and some rock scrambling near the summit.

Place a telephone call to the Taylor Ranch (719-672-3580) before the trip to ascertain access. To write, address your letter to Taylor Ranch, Chama, CO 81126. Permission to climb has varied in recent years, and a fee of $40 per person is currently charged.

Mosquito Range

(5 fourteeners)

Quandary Peak

Mount Lincoln

Mount Democrat

Mount Bross

Mount Sherman

Quandary Peak—14,265 feet

Map—Breckenridge 7.5 M
Rating—Moderate
Elevation gain—3,300 feet
Round-trip distance—6 miles
Estimated round-trip time—6 hours
Nearest town—Breckenridge

Drive through the Eisenhower Tunnel on Interstate 70 and exit at Frisco, heading south on Colorado 9 toward Breckenridge. Continue south past the town for approximately 9 miles to where an improved road, marked 850 (with a sign that looks like a street sign), heads west up a canyon. Immediately thereafter, an unimproved road angles up to the right from County Road 850. Take this road (County Road 851) to a trailhead a little over 1 mile from County Road 850. Park your vehicle in this area. The trail leads west through timber and follows the ridge above timberline over tundra and talus to the summit.

This is a favorite ski climb for winter and spring ascents.

Mount Lincoln—14,286 feet
Mount Democrat—14,148 feet
Mount Bross—14,172

Map—Alma 7.5 M, Climax 7.5 M
Rating—Moderate
Elevation gain—4,300 feet
Round-trip distance—11 miles
Estimated round-trip time—8 hours
Nearest town—Fairplay

Drive on US 285 to Fairplay, then drive north on Colorado 9 for 6 miles to Alma. In the center of town and across the street from a Texaco gas station, turn left (west) and drive 3 miles up Buckskin Creek Road (also called Secondary Forest Route 416) to 11,000 feet. Camp along Buckskin Creek Road if the climb is not a day trip from Denver.

Mount Democrat

Hike northwest up the road for 2.5 miles to Kite Lake and from there follow the trail north 2 miles to the saddle. Climb Democrat 0.5 mile to the southwest. Or, you can climb from below Kite Lake straight to the summit, looking down on Kite Lake to the south.

Mount Lincoln

Return to the saddle described above and climb northeast for another 0.5 mile over Mount Cameron and then an easy 0.5 mile to the summit of Mount Lincoln.

Mount Bross

Return to the Mount Cameron–Lincoln saddle and follow the gentle trail southeast 1 mile to Mount Bross. Return to Kite Lake for 1.5 miles down the west slope of Bross, taking the trail along the ridge. Continue down a couloir to the old road and back to the lake.

Each mountain by itself is not difficult, but climbing the three together makes for a long day. The route given here starts at 11,000 feet to achieve the minimum of 3,000 feet for an accredited climb. Vehicles can be driven up a rough but negotiable road directly to Kite Lake for an easier climb that begins at 12,000 feet. There is a $3 parking fee at Kite Lake during the summer. This climb can be done from Denver in one day.

Mount Sherman—14,036 feet

Map—Mount Sherman 7.5 M
Rating—Moderate
Elevation gain—2,800 feet
Round-trip distance—9 miles
Estimated round-trip time—8 hours
Nearest town—Fairplay

Drive on US 285 to Fairplay, then continue south past the town for about 1 mile. Turn west (right) on Park County Road 18 to Four Mile Creek. Drive 12 miles to the site of Leavick, a ghost town. Park here and find a campsite in the environs if you plan to camp.

Begin hiking on the road, and pass the first mine, the Dauntless. The Day Mine Company of Leadville, which permits climbers to go through its property to the summit, owns the entire mountain.

Hike northwest up the most obvious road to the abandoned Hilltop Mine, then follow a trail up to the saddle between Mount Sheridan and Mount Sherman. Turn north (right) and hike up the ridge about 1 mile to the summit of Mount Sherman.

You can climb Mount Sheridan first for a more interesting trip, then drop to the saddle and continue up the long ridge to the summit of Mount Sherman.

Sawatch Range

(15 fourteeners)

Mount of the Holy Cross
Mount Massive
Mount Elbert
La Plata Peak
Mount Belford
Mount Oxford
Missouri Mountain
Huron Peak
Mount Harvard
Mount Columbia
Mount Yale
Mount Princeton
Mount Antero
Mount Shavano
Tabeguache Mountain

Mount of the Holy Cross— 14,005 feet

Map—Holy Cross 7.5 M, Minturn 7.5 M
Rating—Moderate, but long
Elevation gain—5,400 feet, including 960 on the return leg
Round-trip distance—14 miles
Estimated round-trip time—12 hours
Nearest town—Minturn

From Minturn drive south on US 24 for 3 miles, turn right (southwest) and drive on Forest Service Road 701 for 8.5 miles, passing Tigiwon Campground, to Half Moon Campground at 10,300 feet. Camp in this area.

Hike west 2 miles to Half Moon Pass at 11,600 feet. Descend 1.7 miles and 960 feet to East Cross Creek. Follow the trail west around a small lake 0.5 mile to the ridge and bear south up the ridge for 3 miles to the summit. Be careful on the descent not to drop left (west) into the West Cross Creek drainage. Remain on the north ridge of the mountain until the trail used during the ascent can be clearly identified descending into the trees at timberline.

Mount Massive—14,421 feet

Map—Mount Massive 7.5 M
Rating—Moderate
Elevation gain—4,400 feet
Round-trip distance—13.5 miles
Estimated round-trip time—10 hours
Nearest town—Leadville

From Malta Junction, which is about 3 miles
southwest of Leadville on US 24, drive west on
County Road 300 for 1 mile, then head south on
Forest Road 110 for 5.5 miles to Halfmoon Campground at 10,000 feet. Camp or proceed another
1.5 miles west and park where the Main Range
Trail crosses the road. There are some unimproved campsites in the vicinity.

Take the Main Range Trail north 3 miles to the
Mount Massive trail. Follow this trail through
timber, then into a bowl and on to the northeast
shoulder of the summit. This trail takes you very
close to the summit, but some boulder scrambling
is required near the top.

Mount Elbert—14,433 feet

Map—Mount Elbert 7.5 M,
  Mount Massive 7.5 M
Rating—Moderate
Elevation gain—4,400 feet
Round-trip distance—10 miles
Estimated round-trip time—9 hours
Nearest town—Leadville

From Malta Junction, which is about 3 miles southwest of Leadville on US 24, drive west on County Road 300 for 1 mile, then head south on Forest Road 110 for 5.5 miles to the Halfmoon Campground at 10,000 feet. Camp or proceed another 1.5 miles west and park where the Main Range Trail crosses the road. There are some un-improved campsites in the vicinity.

CFI Recommended Route

Hike south on the Main Range Trail for 2 miles to a well-defined fork in the trail. Turn right (west) at fork and climb 3 miles up a rather steep trail (southwest) to the summit.

Twin Lakes Route

From Colorado 82, take Lake County Road 24. Pass Lakeview and continue for 0.3 mile more. Take an unmarked road straight ahead where Road 24 turns right. Continue on for about 2 miles and park. Hike west on a rough road, which becomes a trail. The trail connects with the Colorado Trail. Watch for a sign for the Mount Elbert Trail that will take you to the summit.

La Plata Peak—14,336 feet

Map—Winfield 7.5 M, Mount Elbert 7.5 M
Rating—More difficult
Elevation gain—3,600 feet
Round-trip distance—10 miles
Estimated round-trip time—9 hours
Nearest town—Leadville

CFI Recommended Route

From Leadville, drive toward Independence Pass on US 24, then turn west (right) onto Colorado 82. Continue for 14.5 miles. Look for a parking area on your left near the South Fork Lake Creek Road. Park here. Hike along South Fork Lake Creek Road, crossing Lake Creek on a good bridge and follow signs to the trailhead. The first mile of the climb passes through private property. Continue through forest and meadow to the ridge at 12,700 feet. Ascend the northwest ridge over talus and across steep rocky slopes. The cairn-marked route will take you to the summit. Descend the same way.

From Winfield

Drive on US 24 south from Leadville, or north from Buena Vista. Turn west on a gravel road running along the north side of Clear Creek Reservoir. Go about 12 miles, driving through Vicksburg (ghost town) to Winfield (ghost town), and, starting at the road junction in Winfield, drive 1.8 miles west along the narrow road up the North Fork of Clear Creek. Park at a point where the road makes a gentle curve to the left and starts a short, gradual descent (cars can go about 1 mile of the 1.8 mile distance). There are some good camping sites in this area. Pick up the road that angles up to the right. Follow this road to a metal gate across the road. Just below the gate look for a trail on the left. This trail leads to a high basin where there are old mining cabins. Follow the trail to the head of the basin, where the trail switchbacks up to La Plata's south ridge, which leads to the summit.

Mount Belford—14,197 feet
Mount Oxford—14,153 feet

Map—Mount Harvard 7.5 M
Rating—Moderate
Elevation gain—4,600 feet to 5,900
Round-trip distance—9 miles to 11
Estimated round-trip time—9 to 11 hours
Nearest town—Buena Vista

CFI Recommended Route

Drive north on US 24 for 15 miles, turn left (west) at Clear Creek Reservoir, then proceed 8 miles to Vicksburg at 9,700 feet. Small and primitive camp areas are along Clear Creek, east and west of Vicksburg. Cross Clear Creek on bridge at Vicksburg and hike south on trail up Missouri Gulch for 2 miles, then continue along the creek until you reach timberline. You will see the route up Belford's northwest shoulder. Continue on the Missouri Gulch trail to the trail junction at 11,650 feet. The route climbs to the summit along a well-constructed trail.

Mount Belford to Mount Oxford

It is customary to climb Oxford with Belford. From the summit of Belford find the trail that descends into the saddle between Belford and Oxford, dropping 700 feet. Continue east-north-east to Oxford. To descend, return to the saddle between Oxford and Belford. Return to Belford's summit via the same route. Descend using the ascent route.

This route entails high altitude and exposed hiking for about a mile in each direction. Check the weather before proceeding since there is no shelter from sudden storms.

These two peaks have a well-deserved reputation for sudden, violent electric storms. Climb them early in the morning.

Missouri Mountain—14,067 feet

Map—Winfield 7.5 M
Rating—More difficult
Elevation gain—4,500 feet
Round-trip distance—9 miles
Estimated round-trip time—8 hours
Nearest town—Buena Vista

Camp as for Belford and Oxford. Cross Clear Creek on the bridge at Vicksburg and hike south on the trail up Missouri Gulch for 3 miles, then select one of the grassy slopes to climb southwest 0.5 mile to the ridge. Do not head toward the rocks in the vicinity of Elkhead Pass since this is a dangerous way to the summit. Once on the ridge, proceed south-southeast along the narrow ridge trail to the summit. There is some exposure along the ridge trail.

Huron Peak—14,005 feet

Map—Winfield 7.5 M
Rating—More difficult
Elevation gain—3,200 feet
Round-trip distance—8.5 miles
Estimated round-trip time—6.5 hours
Nearest town—Buena Vista and Leadville

CFI Recommended Route

Drive on US 24 south from Leadville, or north from Buena Vista. Turn west on a gravel road running along the north side of Clear Creek Reservoir. Go about 12 miles, driving through Vicksburg (ghost town) to Winfield (ghost town).

Begin at the end of the South Fork Clear Creek Road (approximately 2.5 to 3 miles from Winfield and past the old Banker Mine). Park here. Hike south on the South Fork of Clear Creek Trail a short distance to the Huron Peak Trail going off to the left. Follow this unmaintained path up the first small hill. Look to the right (south) for a very faint trail and follow it to a small creek. At the creek, the trail begins to climb steeply to timberline.

From this point, Huron's summit and large basin are plainly visible. Continue on the trail (faint at times) above a grassy plateau into the basin. Hike up through the basin toward Point 13,518 feet, which is located on the connecting ridge between Browns and Huron. Just to the south of Point 13,518 is a small saddle. Reach the saddle and continue on the rocky ridge of Huron's north ridge. Remain on the ridge to the summit, avoiding the large scree and talus bowl.

Remain on the ridge for the descent until you regain the trail.

Mount Harvard—14,420 feet
Mount Columbia—14,073 feet

Map—Mount Harvard 7.5 M
Rating—More difficult
Elevation gain—6,500 feet, both peaks
Round-trip distance—14 miles from cars
Estimated round-trip time—12 hours
Nearest town—Buena Vista

From the center of Buena Vista, drive north 0.4 mile on US 24, then turn left (west) on Chaffee County Road 350 (Crossman Avenue) for 2 miles, then north and northwest 1 mile. At the Forest Service sign "North Cottonwood Creek," turn south for 0.2 mile, then west and northwest for 5 miles to the end of a passable road. Park here and backpack in. After leaving the parking area, the trail crosses a bridge to the south side of the creek and proceeds westward 1.5 miles to a trail junction just after the trail returns to the north side of the creek on a second bridge. Take the right-hand trail marked "Horn Fork Basin" northwest, then west 2.5 miles to timberline. Camp in this area.

Mount Harvard

From camp, follow the trail 1.25 miles to the basin below Mount Harvard. Pass Bear Lake on the trail and continue north up the steep grass and rock ridge. Proceed under the crest of the south shoulder of the summit block, and scramble up large boulders to the summit.

Harvard to Columbia

Follow the east ridge of Harvard to the saddle at 13,440 feet, just west of Point 13,516. Next, drop off the ridge to the east and descend to the creek at 12,200 feet. Head south and a little west up grassy slopes, then over rocks to the summit of Columbia. The descent to the west encounters loose rocks and scree.

Mount Columbia

From camp, hike east under a small set of cliffs. Once clear of the cliffs, climb east up a steep grassy slope to the ridge. Follow the ridge to Mount Columbia's summit.

Mount Yale—14,196 feet

Map—Mount Yale 7.5 M
Rating—More difficult
Elevation gain—4,400 feet
Round-trip distance—8 miles
Estimated round-trip time—8 hours
Nearest town—Buena Vista

From Buena Vista drive west on Chaffee County Road 306 along Middle Cottonwood Creek for 12 miles. Park near the Denny Creek trailhead and sign the register (right side of the road). You will be following a wide trail and will make two creek crossings. When you reach a fork, bear right and proceed northwest for 0.25 mile to an intersection that should be marked. Take the right fork into Delaney Gulch. Follow the trail to the south ridge and continue along the ridge to the summit. Descend the way you came.

Mount Princeton—14,197 feet

Map—Mount Antero 7.5 M,
Buena Vista West 7.5 M
Rating—Moderate
Elevation gain—3,200 feet
Round-trip distance—6 miles from cars
Estimated round-trip time—7 hours
Nearest town—Buena Vista

From Buena Vista drive south on US 285 for 8 miles, then turn west on County Road 162 to Chalk Creek Road. Turn right at Mount Princeton Hot Springs Inn. Continue up along the road through the Young Life Camp and follow the road as far as the TV relay station at 10,800 feet. How passable this road is depends on the vehicle and the season. There is a good campsite where the stream branches.

Hike along the road for about 1 to 1.5 miles beyond the TV relay station to where the road emerges from timber, just short of the boulder field. From this point, the A-frame Young Life chalet is visible. About 100 yards farther, a trail leaves the road uphill to the right. The trailhead is not obvious unless you go too far and look back. Follow this good trail until you are within 0.2 mile or less of the mine at its end. Cut left, up to a ridge that offers good access to the summit along a rocky, but usually dry, route.

Mount Antero—14,269 feet

Map—Mount Antero 7.5 M, St. Elmo 7.5 M
Rating—Moderate
Elevation gain—3,300 feet
Round-trip distance—7 miles
Estimated round-trip time—8 hours
Nearest town—Buena Vista

From Buena Vista drive south on US 285 for 8 miles, then turn west on County Road 162 for 9.5 miles to Cascade Campground. Camp here, and in the morning, drive another 2 miles west on County Road 162 to Baldwin Gulch Road at 9,239 feet. Turn left (south) and follow rugged Baldwin Gulch Road for 3 miles to a creek crossing, at about 11,000 feet. This road is for jeeps. Cross the creek and follow the road until it begins to switch-back up the broad slopes above you. Follow a convenient gully to by-pass the road and gain the south ridge of the peak. You may also stay on the road to just short of the summit.

Quartz, aquamarine and topaz crystals are common in this area and you may come across geologists and miners who have driven up to near the summit on the jeep road.

The final ascent is up a trail through talus.

Mount Shavano—14,229 feet
Tabeguache Mountain—14,155 feet

Map—St. Elmo 7.5 M, Mount Antero 7.5 M,
  Garfield 7.5 M, Maysville 7.5 M
Rating—More difficult
Elevation gain—3,800 feet to Tabeguache,
  500 feet to Shavano
Round-trip distance—8 miles
Estimated round-trip time—8 to 9 hours
Nearest town—Buena Vista

From US 285 at Poncha Junction, drive west on
US 50 for 6 miles to Maysville. Turn right (north)
and follow the North Fork approximately 8 miles
to Jennings Creek, which is 1.7 miles past Shavano Campground. Parking may be limited at Jennings Creek. However, there is adequate parking
0.25 mile west and on the left.

Tabeguache Mountain

Find a trail on the east side of the road where
Jennings Creek intersects it at 10,522 feet. This
trail may be difficult to find at first as it is ob-
scured by aspen trees and undergrowth. Hike
north for 0.5 mile, then northeast up loose dirt
and scree to the ridge. You will pass through an
old burn area. Follow this broad ridge to 13,908
feet and continue east 0.5 mile to the summit.

Shavano Peak

From the summit of Tabeguache, drop east to the saddle at 13,700, then continue southeast, gaining 500 or more feet to Shavano's summit. For the descent, drop into upper McCoy Creek basin, traversing high, then climb up and over the Tabeguache ridge and back down the trail to Jennings Creek. Do not attempt to follow McCoy Creek down. It drops steeply into an increasingly narrow canyon and you can get trapped with no descent option but to retrace your steps.

Elk Range
(6 fourteeners)

Capitol Peak
Snowmass Mountain
North Maroon Peak
Maroon (South Maroon) Peak
Pyramid Peak
Castle Peak

Capitol Peak—14,130 feet

Map—Capitol Peak 7.5 M
Rating—Difficult, climbing helmet &
  rope needed
Elevation gain—3,800 feet
Round-trip distance—17 miles
Estimated round-trip time—12 hours
Nearest town—Aspen

From Aspen, drive 14 miles northwest on Colorado 82 to the Snowmass Post Office. Then drive south almost 2 miles. Keep right at the fork and continue less than 0.5 mile to the next fork. There, keep left. Continue 1.5 miles southwest to another fork. Take the right fork. (The left fork leads to St. Benedict Monastery.) Follow the road for approximately 4 miles to an area where there are several cabins (in the vicinity of Capitol Creek Guard Station) to the right of the road. Most passenger cars should be able to drive another 1.5 miles to a meadow at 9,400 feet. The Capitol Creek Trail drops 400 feet to the left of the meadow, but a jeep road leaves the upper end of the meadow to Williams Lake and Hardscrabble Lake. At the point where the jeep road crosses a ditch on a bridge, there is a trail that follows the ditch to the left of the road. This trail joins the Capitol Creek Trail without the 400-foot loss in elevation, but you may encounter a problematic stream crossing, especially during runoff, before you can rejoin the trail.

Backpack from the meadow south for 6.5 miles

along the Capitol Creek Trail to the north end of Capitol Lake at 11,600 feet. Camp here. Follow all Forest Service regulations when you camp since camping rules are enforced vigorously in this area.

From the lake, the Capitol Creek Trail climbs east 0.5 mile to the Capitol-Daly ridge. Drop several hundred feet on the east side of the ridge and climb up the basin to the point where the ridges on either side merge just before the knife edge. After crossing the knife edge, do an ascending traverse across Capitol's south face, following cairns, to gain the northeast ridge. Follow the ridge to the summit.

Watch the weather constantly. The ridge is exposed, and lightning storms are frequent from April to September.

Snowmass Mountain—14,092 feet

**Map—Snowmass Mountain 7.5 M,
  Capitol Peak 7.5 M**
**Rating—More difficult or very difficult,
  depending on route**
Elevation gain—5,700 feet
Round-trip distance—22 miles
Estimated round-trip time—16 hours
Nearest town—Aspen

From Aspen, drive 14 miles on Colorado 82 to the
Snowmass Post Office. Turn left (south) into
Snowmass Creek Road. After almost 2 miles, at
the T-junction, keep left and continue along
Snowmass Creek Road to Snowmass Falls Ranch.
This ranch can also be reached from Snowmass
Village over a rough but short pass, usable by pas-
senger cars. This is a shorter route to the ranch.
There is a parking lot near the ranch, but not a
campground.

From Snowmass Lake

Backpack south 9 miles, gaining 2,600 feet in ele-
vation, up Snowmass Creek to Snowmass Lake at
11,000 feet. Camp on the east side of the lake.
From this approach the whole of Snowmass
Mountain is in view to the right of Hagerman
Peak.

Hike 0.2 mile around the south shore of the
lake and climb west into the basin, keeping to the
right (north) of Hagerman Peak. Then, climb onto
the ridge between Hagerman and Snowmass and

follow the southeast ridge to the summit. This is a moderate but long ascent.

From Marble

From Marble, use the four-wheel-drive road to Lead King Basin, which is on the way to Crystal. Take a left at a sign marked "Lead King Basin." Park at 9,700 feet where there is also camping. Hike north on an obvious trail to Siberia Lake, passing Geneva and Gem lakes. Hike east up a steep couloir on the north side of the summit, which is very steep and loose. Do not try to return to Marble via Crystal. The road is very bad.

North Maroon Peak—14,014 feet
Maroon (South Maroon) Peak—14,156 feet
Pyramid Peak—14,018 feet

Map—Maroon Bells 7.5 M

Rating—Very difficult, climbing helmet & rope for all three

Elevation gain—4,400 feet

Round-trip distance—8 miles for North Maroon Peak, 10 miles for South Maroon Peak, 7 miles for Pyramid Peak

Estimated round-trip time—11 hours for North Maroon Peak, 12 hours for South Maroon Peak, 10 hours for Pyramid Peak

Nearest town—Aspen

The Maroon Bells and Pyramid, which are among Colorado's most picturesque peaks, are also the most dangerous. The primary hazard of loose and falling rock can be somewhat minimized by climbing in small parties and during the week, not on weekends.

There are three Maroon Bells, but climbing instructions for only two are provided here. The third is the 13,753-foot appendage south of Maroon Peak (or South Maroon Peak). The route described below for climbing South Maroon will take the climber very near, if not over, this summit.

From Aspen, drive northwest 1.2 miles on Colorado 82 and turn left (south). Keep right at the fork that appears immediately on the road to

Maroon Lake. Drive about 9 miles to the end of the road. There may be a new designated parking lot for climbers. During the summer months, access to Maroon Lake has been restricted mostly to buses. The Forest Service office in Aspen will have schedules of bus departures and also any changes in access to this very popular area. It is best to call the Aspen Ranger District Office, White River National Forest, at (970) 925-3445, to obtain the latest regulations.

North Maroon Peak

Take the trail past Maroon Lake to Crater Lake (about 1.5 miles); then take the right fork of the trail toward Buckskin Pass. Near timberline (about 1 mile above Crater Lake), drop to the left of the trail and camp near the stream, at 11,100 feet. From camp, drop west across a gully and stream and climb southwest 0.75 mile to a timberline bench. There is a definite trail across this bench. Pass through a grassy couloir and head southeast to a rock glacier under the north face of North Maroon. Contour south around the east ridge into a second, wide couloir with rocky benches. Climb up this couloir for about 0.3 mile. This will entail climbing through a white band of rock halfway up the distance. There is a cleft in what otherwise is a small cliff. Eventually, this couloir runs into the summit ridge at 13,500 feet. Cross this ridge to the north face. Proceed west to a hard chimney on the north side of the ridge. The chimney can be climbed with a basic amount of technical knowledge. Climb west along the ridge to the summit. Cairns mark this route; alternate trails are more exposed and subject to frequent rock falls.

Maroon (South Maroon) Peak

Take the trail past Maroon Lake to Crater Lake, keeping left (not *right* as above in the North Maroon instructions) at the fork overlooking Crater Lake. Continue approximately 1 mile beyond Crater Lake along the west side of West Maroon Creek to the point where the trail crosses the creek near timberline. Do not cross the creek. Instead, leave the trail and angle southwest, to the right of the stream, up steep, loose, grassy slopes to the ridge. This is a long climb, gaining 2,800 feet. Turn right (north) and follow the ridge to the summit, keeping left (west) where the crest of the ridge is formidable. Much of the route is marked with cairns.

Pyramid Peak

Take the trail past Maroon Lake toward Crater Lake. After about 1 mile, you will reach a rocky area marked by cairns. Before reaching Crater Lake, cross the valley to the southeast on a moraine. Climb steeply up the slope to the low point of the large basin north of the peak.

Once well into the basin, two routes are possible:

- For larger parties, the northeast ridge route is better. To follow this route, climb directly out of the basin to the lowest saddle on the east skyline, then keep on the southeast side of the ridge and follow it to the summit.

- Smaller groups can proceed from the basin steeply up to the obvious saddle on the northwest ridge of the peak. From there, climb up and south to approach the summit from the south. This route has significant exposure.

Castle Peak—14,265 feet

Map—Hayden Peak 7.5 M
Rating—More difficult
Elevation gain—4,400 feet
Round-trip distance—13 miles
Estimated round-trip time—12 hours
Nearest town—Aspen

This peak is the highest, but also the easiest to climb in the Elk Range. From Aspen, drive northwest 1 mile on Colorado 82, then turn left (south) and take an immediate left-hand road to Ashcroft for 12 miles. Continue for 2 miles beyond Ashcroft. Turn right onto the smaller Pearl Pass Road, as the main road continues straight ahead and crosses Castle Creek. After another 0.5 mile, the road starts to climb at 9,900 feet. If using a conventional vehicle, park and camp in aspen groves.

Either hike or use a four-wheel-drive vehicle to ascend about 2.5 miles to 11,000 feet to the Pearl Pass Road junction, which is unmarked. Turn right and follow the Montezuma Mine Road to the end, which is well over 12,000 feet.

One route is to climb from the end of the Montezuma Mine Road by heading southwest up the valley. At 13,400 feet, head south to gain the northeast ridge of Castle Peak. Follow the ridge to the summit. Descend by the same route, or descend the northwest ridge to the saddle between Castle Peak and Conundrum Peak. When snow is abundant, a long, exhilarating glissade is possible from the Conundrum saddle.

San Juan Range

(13 fourteeners)

San Luis Peak

Uncompahgre Peak

Wetterhorn Peak

Redcloud Peak

Sunshine Peak

Handies Peak

Windom Peak

Sunlight Peak

Mount Eolus

Mount Sneffels

Wilson Peak

Mount Wilson

El Diente

San Luis Peak—14,014 feet

Map—San Luis Peak 7.5 M,
  Stewart Peak 7.5 M
Rating—Moderate
Elevation gain—3,600 feet
Round-trip distance—10 miles
Estimated round-trip time—10 hours
Nearest town—Gunnison

The challenge in climbing this peak is to reach the Stewart Creek trailhead.

Drive 8 miles east of Gunnison on US 50 and turn south onto State Road 114 (The Cochetopa Canyon Road). Follow it for 17 miles. Turn right onto Forest Road 3083. The distance from this intersection to the trailhead is about another 30 miles. Pick up these Forest Roads in succession: 3084, 788, 790, 794.28 and 794. A Gunnison Basin Forest Service map is very valuable in finding and following these roads. You can purchase the map at the Cimarron Ranger Station, 216 North Colorado, Gunnison, CO 81230, or you can send a check for $4 (paper map) or $6 (plastic map) to get the map by mail. The station's telephone number is (970) 641-0471.

Forest Road 794 dead ends at Stewart Creek—park here. There are numerous campsites in this area.

Pick up the trailhead at the dead end of the road and hike west up Stewart Creek Valley, keeping to the right (north) side of the creek at all times. At the end of the valley you will see a high, flattened pyramid–shaped peak. After climbing past several gulches coming in from the left, ascend to the saddle on the northwest slope of San Luis Peak. From this point, the summit can be seen 0.2 mile away in a west, southwest direction, but it is still a long hike.

Uncompahgre Peak—14,309 feet
Wetterhorn Peak—14,017 feet

Map—Wetterhorn Peak 7.5 M,
  Uncompahgre Peak 7.5 M
Rating—More difficult
Elevation gain—3,900 feet for Uncompahgre;
  3,600 for Wetterhorn; 5,500 feet for both
Round-trip distance—11 miles for
  Uncompahgre; 8 for Wetterhorn; 15 for both
Estimated round-trip time—9 hours for
  Uncompahgre; 7 for Wetterhorn; 13 for both
Nearest town—Lake City

From Lake City, pick up Henson Creek Road (look for Engineer Pass sign) and drive 10 miles west and 1.5 miles northwest to a campground near Matterhorn Creek at 10,400 feet. The road is permanently closed to vehicles a short distance above the camp.

Uncompahgre Peak from Matterhorn Creek

Hike north for 3 miles along the road to Matterhorn Creek and a pass at 12,458 feet. Continue east on the road across the basin. The road passes south of the peak, then becomes a trail that doubles back west, then north, to the summit. It is shorter and easier to leave the road south-southwest of the peak, in a relatively flat area with several ponds, and head across the basin. Work up the grassy slopes of the south ridge. You will be climbing to the right of Point 13,018 feet (shown on the map) and will re-join the trail above

13,000 feet. Continue to the summit, 2.5 miles from the pass.

On the descent, follow the trail back to about 13,300 feet, then pick a route down the steep slopes to Point 13,018 feet. Return to the basin and continue southwest back to the road.

Uncompahgre Peak from Nellie Creek

In Lake City find County Road 20 and drive west for about 5 miles. Turn north (right) onto the Nellie Creek Road. You can drive to about 11,000 feet here with a passenger car, although the road has steep switchbacks and can be slippery during wet weather when a four-wheel-drive vehicle is advisable. Park at the end of the road and find the clearly marked trail that takes you to Uncompahgre's summit.

Wetterhorn from Matterhorn Creek

Hike north for 2 miles along the road to Matterhorn Creek to a spring that is marked on the map. Leave the road, cross to the west side of the creek, and follow it north. Head west up the ridge, past Point 13,117 feet, which is marked on the map. Continue along the left side of the ridge. Work up on the west side of the peak to the summit on a system of ledges.

The route appears to be very steep and formidable, but it goes well if the trail is dry.

Wetterhorn and Uncompahgre Peaks Together

Both peaks can be climbed in one day by a reasonably strong party. Climb Wetterhorn Peak, then descend southeast down the ridge. Pick a route on grassy areas and traverse east as far as possible, south of Matterhorn Peak. This will enable you to intersect the road to the pass, then follow the route to Uncompahgre Peak. This is a very long climb.

Redcloud Peak—14,034 feet
Sunshine Peak—14,001 feet

Map—Redcloud Peak 7.5 M
Rating—More difficult
Elevation gain—3,600 feet, plus 500 feet
Round-trip distance—8 miles
Estimated round-trip time—8 hours
Nearest town—Lake City

From Lake City, drive approximately 15 miles up the Lake Fork of the Gunnison River on County Road 30. Take the right-hand fork onto County Road 4 toward Cinnamon Pass and drive for just over 4 miles to Grizzly Creek at 10,400 feet. There is an excellent campsite near Grizzly Gulch in the area of Silver Creek with water (not potable) and an outhouse.

Using the standard cairn route, hike northeast up the trail 2 miles to the northwest side of Silver Creek. Continue on the trail along the creek. At timberline, cross the creek, gain the saddle north of Redcloud, and climb the ridge southeast for 1 mile to the summit of Redcloud.

Sunshine Peak

Follow the Redcloud ridge south 1.5 miles. You will drop 500 feet between peaks. After reaching Sunshine, drop back to the saddle and return via Redcloud Peak, unless weather and lightning require that you get off the ridge.

The alternate descent is from the saddle between the peaks. Drop to the west over rough talus and scree until you reach the Silver Creek Trail.

Handies Peak—14,048 feet

Map—Handies Peak 7.5 M,
Redcloud Peak 7.5 M
Rating—Moderate
Elevation gain—3,600 feet
Round-trip distance—7 miles
Estimated round-trip time—5 hours
Nearest town—Lake City

From Lake City, drive approximately 15 miles up the Lake Fork of the Gunnison River on County Road 30. Take the right-hand fork onto County Road 4 toward Cinnamon Pass and drive for just over 4 miles to Grizzly Creek at 10,400 feet. There is an excellent campsite near Grizzly Gulch in the area of Silver Creek with water (not potable) and an outhouse.

Cross the Lake Fork of the Gunnison River and hike up the Grizzly Gulch Trail north out of the valley and west to the ridge. From the ridge it is an easy climb south to the summit.

From American Basin

An easier, 4-to-5-hour round trip climb that has an elevation gain of only 2,700 feet is possible from the American Basin. Continue south on Cinnamon Pass Road for about 3.5 miles past Grizzly Creek. Take a four-wheel-drive road heading south into the American Basin. Park along this road. Follow the road as it changes into a trail and begins to climb up grassy slopes. Continue south and west to the south ridge of Handies, then to the summit. Return by the same route, following the trail.

Windom Peak—14,082 feet
Sunlight Peak—14,059 feet
Mount Eolus—14,083 feet

**Maps—Mountain View Crest 7.5 M,
  Columbine Pass 7.5 M, Storm King
  Peak 7.5 M**
Rating—Very difficult, rope needed
Elevation gain—3,100 to 3,700 feet
**Round-trip distance—3 to 6 miles from
  Chicago Basin**
**Estimated round-trip time—5 to 8 hours from
  Chicago Basin**
Nearest town—Durango

Windom and Sunlight are close together with little elevation loss on the route connecting them.
They should be climbed on the same day, unless
weather dictates otherwise.

To reach the trailhead, take the Durango and
Silverton Railroad from Durango to Needleton at
8,212 feet. The train runs to Silverton and back
daily during the summer. Make advance reserva-
tions for the train, which is a popular tourist
attraction, by writing to the railroad at 479 Main
Avenue, Durango, CO 81301, or by calling (970)
247-2733. Or take your chances as a standby.
When you disembark, cross the river on the sus-
pension bridge and backpack east 7.2 miles up the
trail along Needle Creek. Camp in Chicago Basin
at about 11,000 feet in the area where the trail
crosses to the south bank of Needle Creek and
starts up Columbine Pass.

Windom Peak

Follow Needle Creek and a good trail north 1 mile to Twin Lakes at 12,500 feet. Turn east up the large basin between Sunlight and Windom. Keep to the left of Peak 13,472 (Peak 18), the dominant feature on the ascent. Continue east 0.2 mile and climb southeast to the west ridge of Windom at 13,250 feet near the Peak 18-Windom Peak col, a depression in the crest of the ridge. Continue east along the ridge 0.2 mile to the summit.

Sunlight Peak

From Chicago Basin, follow the trail north to Twin Lakes. Turn east into the basin between Sunlight and Peak 13,995. Climb gradually up to the connecting ridge between Sunlight and Windom. Turn north (left) to Sunlight Peak. You will traverse the northwest shoulder of Peak 13,995. Then continue northwest up Sunlight's ridge to the summit. A rope is recommended for anyone climbing the last 10 feet to the true summit. It is a long way down to the north.

An alternative route is to climb north up the couloir nearly to the col on the west of Sunlight. From here, easy ledges lead to just below the west ridge and on to the foot of the summit block.

Mount Eolus

Use the same trail as described for Sunlight to hike toward Twin Lakes from Chicago Basin. Before you get to Twin Lakes, head west. As you approach the great east face of Eolus, head northeast up a slab to the saddle between Eolus and Glacier Point at 13,700 feet. Turn west to the saddle between Eolus and North Eolus. Traverse southwest across a narrow and exposed ridge that enjoys the names "Sidewalk in the Sky" and "Catwalk." The ridge terminates in the east face of Eolus. Use the ledges on the face, keeping to the left and taking care to select the route, to ascend to the summit.

Mount Sneffels—14,150 feet

Maps—Mount Sneffels 7.5 M, Telluride 7.5 M
Rating—More difficult
Elevation gain—3,400 feet
Round-trip distance—6 miles
Estimated round-trip time—5 to 6 hours
Nearest town—Ouray

From US 550, 0.5 mile south of Ouray, turn right and drive 6.5 miles. The Yankee Boy Basin Road bears to the right all the way to its end. Drive to timberline and park.

Follow the Yankee Boy Basin Road up Yankee Boy Basin, famous for its alpine wildflowers and hummingbirds, to its end, then pick up the Blue Lake Pass Trail. Follow this trail to 12,700 feet, then head northeast, traversing around a boulder field to gain a wide couloir. The couloir leads to a saddle at 13,500 feet. Turn northwest on the saddle and enter a narrower and steeper rock-filled couloir that leads up to the wall under the summit. Before reaching the end of this couloir, look for another much smaller and shorter couloir and take it. It leads to the left and terminates in a V-shaped notch through which you can climb out onto the approach to the summit, about 100 yards above.

If either of these couloirs becomes too difficult because of snow, it may be possible to move out of them to the west and approach the summit across the southwest face of Sneffels.

Wilson Peak—14,017 feet

Maps—Little Cone 7.5 M, Gray Head 7.5 M
Delores Peak 7.5 M, Mount Wilson 7.5 M
Rating—Very difficult, climbing helmet needed
Elevation gain—3,350 feet
Round-trip distance—6 miles
Estimated round-trip time—10 hours
Nearest town—Placerville

From Placerville, drive 7 miles southeast to Vanadium on Colorado 145. Turn right up Big Bear Creek. At 2.5 miles south of Vanadium, keep right. At 4 miles, take the center choice of three roads. At about 6 miles, the road is blocked to further vehicle travel. You may car camp here (no water) or backpack 2 miles to the Silver Pick Mine and camp where there is water.

Follow the trail into Silver Pick Basin west of Wilson Peak and up to the saddle at 13,000 feet. Contour around the southwest side of the peak, heading slightly south to gain a saddle at 13,280 feet on the south ridge of Wilson Peak. Continue northeast to gain the summit, picking the route carefully along the ridge. The rock can be very loose here.

Mount Wilson—14,246 feet

Maps—Gray Head 7.5 M, Delores Peak 7.5 M
Rating—Very difficult, climbing helmet, ice
    axe & rope needed
Elevation gain—5,200 feet
Round-trip distance—15 miles
Estimated round-trip time—15 hours
Nearest town—Telluride and Rico

To approach Mount Wilson from Navajo Basin, drive south on Colorado 145 for 5.5 miles beyond Lizard Head Pass. Turn right (west) on Dunton Road (Forest Road 535). Follow Dunton Road for 6 miles, past Morgan Camp, to Forest Road 207. Then turn right for 0.2 mile on a short road that terminates in a parking area at West Dolores River. The Navajo Lake trailhead is located at the northern end of the parking area. Follow the trail north along the river for 5 miles to Navajo Lake, where there are campsites east of the lake.

Climb east to the head of Navajo Basin. At 12,300 feet, turn south and follow the ridge on the western side between Gladstone and Mount Wilson. This should enable you to skirt the permanent snowfield along the way. At 13,800 feet, head southwest to gain the northeast ridge of Mount Wilson. At 14,100 feet, head south through a notch in the ridge. This leads to a dramatic, exposed ridge that culminates in the summit. Descend using the same route.

You can also climb Mount Wilson by using the

Kilpacker Creek approach described with El Diente. If you select this route, then Mount Wilson and El Diente can be summitted the same day.

El Diente—14,159 feet

Maps—Delores Peak 7.5 M,
  Mount Wilson 7.5 M
Rating—Very difficult, climbing helmet, ice
  axe & rope needed
Elevation gain—4,100 feet
Round-trip distance—13 miles
Estimated round-trip time—12 hours
Nearest town—Telluride

From Telluride drive on Colorado 145 east, then south over Lizard Head Pass until you reach Dunton Road (Forest Road 535). Drive west on Dunton Road. After about 5.5 miles, as Dunton Road begins to lose altitude, turn right onto a small road that passes through a meadow. Continue for another 0.25 mile to a grove of trees where there is limited parking. Hike on this closed, jeep road north and northeast for another 1.5 miles to Kilpacker Creek. Do not cross the creek. Just south of the creek, pick up a trail heading east and continue generally up along the creek after the trail crosses the creek and ends. Pass two waterfalls near timberline. Continue up the drainage to gain the Mount Wilson–El Diente ridge. Gain the ridge to the left, or west, of a formation called the Organ Pipes. This route eliminates a difficult traverse around the formation. As you head for the summit, switch to the north side of the ridge.

This is a difficult, dangerous and challenging

climb. It is strongly advised that you consult more detailed guides and carry the appropriate maps and equipment.

COLORADO FOURTEENERS RANKED BY HEIGHT

MOUNTAIN	PAGE	ALTITUDE	RANK	QUADRANGLE	RANGE
Mount Elbert	44	14,433	1	Mt. Elbert 7.5M	Sawatch
				Mount Massive 7.5M	
Mount Massive	43	14,421	2	Mt. Massive 7.5M	Sawatch
Mount Harvard	53	14,420	3	Mt. Harvard 7.5M	Sawatch
Blanca Peak	31	14,345	4	Blanca Peak 7.5M	Sangre de Crisco
				Twin Peaks 7.5M	
La Plata Peak	46	14,336	5	Mt. Elbert 7.5 M	Sawaatch
				Winfield 7.5M	
Uncompahgre Peak	74	14,309	6	Wetterhorn Peak 7.5M	San Juan
				Uncompahgre Peak 7.5M	
Crestone Peak	26	14,294	7	Crestone Peak 7.5M	Sangre de Cristo
Mount Lincoln	37	14,286	8	Alma 7.5M	Mosquito
				Climax 7.5M	
Grays Peak	16	14,270	9	Grays Peak 7.5M	Front
Mount Antero	57	14,269	10	Mount Antero 7.5M	Sawatch
				St. Elmo 7.5M	
Tzorreys Peak	16	14,267	11	Grays Peak 7.5M	Front
Castle Peak	70	14,265	12	Hayden Peak 7.5M	Elk Mountains

Peak	No.	Elevation	Map No.	Quad	Range
Quandary Peak	36	14,265	13	Breckenridge 7.5M	Mosquito
Mount Evans	18	14,264	14	Mt. Evans 7.5M	Front
				Idaho Springs 7.5M	Front
Longs Peak	14	14,255	15	Longs Peak 7.5M	Front
Mount Wilson	86	14,246	16	Gray Head 7.5M	San Juan
				Delores Peak 7.5M	
Mount Shavano	58	14,229	17	St. Elmo 7.5M	Sawatch
				Mount Antero 7.5M	
				Garfield 7.5M	
				Maysville 7.5M	
Mount Princeton	56	14,197	18	Mount Antero 7.5M	Sawatch
				Buena Vista West 7.5M	
Mount Belford	48	14,197	19	Mt. Harvard 7.5M	Sawatch
Mount Yale	55	14,196	20	Mt. Yale 7.5M	Sawatch
Crestone Needle	27	14,191	21	Crestone Peak 7.5M	Sangre de Cristo
Mount Bross	38	14,172	22	Alma 7.5M	Mosquito
				Climax 7.5M	
Kit Carson Peak	24	14,165	23	Crestone Peak 7.5M	Sangre de Cristo
El Diente	88	14,159	24	Dolores Peak 7.5M	San Juan
				Mt. Wilson 7.5M	

(continues)

Fourteeners (continued)

MOUNTAIN	PAGE	ALTITUDE	RANK	QUADRANGLE	RANGE
Maroon Peak	66	14,156	25	Maroon Bells 7.5M	Elk
Tabeguache Mtn.	58	14,155	26	St. Elmo 7.5M	Sawatch
				Mount Antero 7.5M	
				Garfield 7.5M	
				Maysville 7.5M	
Mount Oxford	48	14,153	27	Mt. Harvard 7.5M	Sawatch
Mount Sneffels	84	14,150	28	Mt. Sneffels 7.5M	San Juan
				Telluride 7.5M	
Mount Democrat	37	14,148	29	Alma 7.5M	Mosquito
				Climax 7.5M	
Capitol Peak	62	14,130	30	Capitol Peak 7.5M	Elk Mountains
Pikes Peak	21	14,110	31	Pikes Peak 7.5M	Front
Snowmass Mountain	64	14,092	32	Snowmass Mountain 7.5M	Elk
Mount Eolus	81	14,083	33	Mountain View Crest 7.5M	San Juan
				Columbine Pass 7.5M	
				Storm King Peak 7.5M	

Peak	No.	Elevation		Quadrangle Map	Range
Windom Peak	81	14,082	34	Mountain View Crest 7.5M	San Juan
				Columbine Pass 7.5M	
				Storm King Peak 7.5M	
Mount Columbia	53	14,073	35	Mt. Harvard 7.5M	Sawatch
Culebra Peak	33	14,069	36	Culebra Peak 7.5M	Sangre de Cristo
				El Valle Creek 7.5M	
Missouri Mountain	50	14,067	37	Winfield 7.5M	Sawatch
Humboldt Peak	25	14,064	38	Crestone Peak 7.5M	Sangre de Cristo
Mount Bierstadt	20	14,060	39	Mt. Evans 7.5M	Front
Sunlight Peak	81	14,059	40	Mountain View Crest 7.5M	San Juan
Handies Peak	79	14,048	41	Handies Peak 7.5M	San Juan
				Redcloud Peak 7.5M	
Ellingwood Peak	31	14,042	42	Blanca Peak 7.5M	Sangre de Cristo
				Twin Peaks 7.5M	
Mount Lindsey (aka "Old Baldy")	29	14,042	43	Blanca Peak 7.5M	Sangre de Cristo
				Mosca Pass 7.5M	
Little Bear Peak	31	14,037	44	Blanca Peak 7.5M	Sangre de Cristo
				Twin Peaks 7.5M	
Mount Sherman	39	14,036	45	Mt. Sherman 7.5M	Mosquito
				Columbine Pass 7.5M	
				Storm King Peak 7.5M	

(continues)

Fourteeners (continued)

MOUNTAIN	PAGE	ALTITUDE	RANK	QUADRANGLE	RANGE
Redcloud Peak	77	14,034	46	Redcloud Peak 7.5M	San Juan
Pyramid Peak	66	14,018	47	Maroon Bells 7.5M	Elk
Wilson Peak	85	14,017	48	Little Cone 7.5M	San Juan
				Gray Head 7.5M	
				Delores Peak 7.5M	
				Mount Wilson 7.5M	
Wetterhorn Peak	74	14,017	49	Wetterhorn Peak 7.5M	San Juan
				Uncompahgre Peak 7.5M	
North Maroon Peak	66	14,014	50	Maroon Bells 7.5M	Elk
San Luis Peak	72	14,014	51	San Luis Peak 7.5M	San Juan
				Stewart Peak 7.5M	
Huron Peak	51	14,005	52	Winfield 7.5M	Sawatch
Mount of the Holy Cross	42	14,005	53	Holy Cross 7.5M	Sawatch
				Minturn 7.5M	
Sunshine Peak	77	14,001	54	Redcloud Peak 7.5M	San Juan

ALPHABETICAL INDEX

CLIMBER'S JOURNAL

Mtn.	Date	Remarks

CLIMBER'S JOURNAL

Mtn.	Date	Remarks

CLIMBER'S JOURNAL

Mtn.	Date	Remarks

CLIMBER'S JOURNAL

Mtn.	Date	Remarks